D1539391

SUNDAY
MORNING
ALIVE!
B O O K T W O

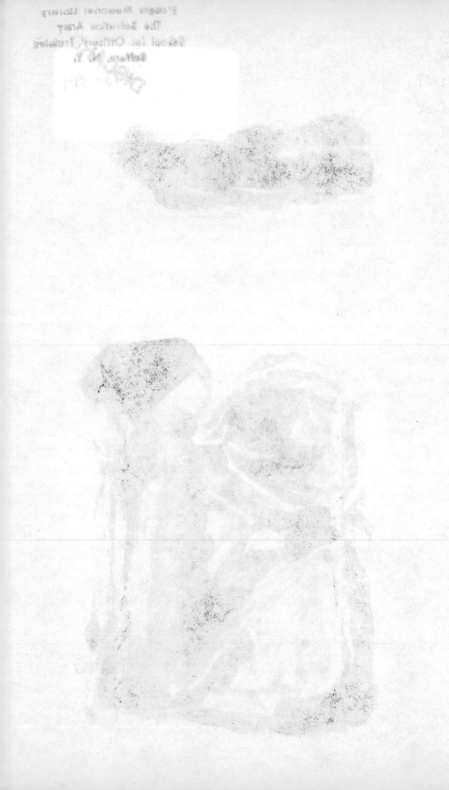

SUNDAY MORNING ALIVE!

B O O K   T W O

170 Ways to Enliven your Worship Service

Shirley Pollock

C.S.S. Publishing Co., Inc.

Lima, Ohio

SUNDAY MORNING ALIVE! BOOK TWO

Library of Congress Cataloging-in-Publication Data

(Revised for volume 2)

Pollock, Shirley E., 1913-
    Sunday morning alive!

    Contents: v. 2. 170 ways to enliven your worship service.
    1. Public worship. I. Title.
BV15.P65 1987   264   87-18227
ISBN 0-89536-887-0 (v. 1)
ISBN 1-55673-069-1 (v. 2)

8866 / ISBN 1-55673-069-1
PRINTED IN U.S.A.

To my husband,
The Reverend James Russell Pollock, PhD., D.D.

Contents

Editor's Preface

Sunday Morning Alive! Book II is the second in a two volume resource library providing 230 stories and descriptions of ways that parishioners and pastors can enhance the worship service and their ministries to the people of their communities. Continuing the style of the previous book, this second volume includes 170 vignettes and descriptions ready for the pastor or worship planner to adapt for use in his or her congregation.

Introduction

Sunday Morning Alive! Book II presents 170 innovative ideas that inject life and enthusiasm into corporate worship. Already tried by various congregations, they adapt to either contemporary or traditional services.

Church-hopping sparked this resource book. I took notes while visiting some two hundred churches of a dozen denominations, in as many states. I recorded all daring and different procedures. I also included personal reactions.

During these ecumenical exposures, I suddenly realized I had something unique to share with pastors, church staff, musicians, lay leaders, and church members. Along with novel, workable ideas, I can present the pew point of view.

That's what makes this book different. It focuses on today's worship, *according to the person in the pew.*

So don't expect scholarly jargon or stained-glass speech. These pages relate eye-witness accounts in the vernacular. I was there. I saw. I heard. I reacted. In addition, some colleagues have given me permission to include what excited them.

Granted, what is innovative for one church may be routine in another. And because these ideas come from so many different denominations, they include evangelical, mainline, liturgical, and charismatic concepts — all in one book. Because of this all-inclusion, you may find procedures that go counter to your church's beliefs and practices. No problem. Like a smorgasbord, pass by what you cannot use; enjoy all you can.

And whether you adapt twenty-two or one-hundred, may your worshipers discover God and express the good news of the Gospel in these different ways to worship. Thus you will celebrate *Sunday Morning Alive!*

Shirley Pollock

Author's Preface

I have lived in parsonages most of my life. My husband is a minister, as was my father.

My religious education, beyond the local church level, included many religious courses at Garret Theological Seminary and Northwestern University, while I attended the School of Speech. Later I audited Church History at Yale Divinity School and attended New College convocations and lectures in Edinburgh, Scotland, while my husband was working on his Ph.D. During those years I typed several doctoral dissertations in religion. One, 880 pages on Saint Augustine, I remember well. From those painstaking labors I must have received some religious insight through osmosis.

Then came years as a minister's wife — helping raise our four daughters, listening eagerly to my husband's sermons every Sunday, and involving myself in all phases of church and community services. As a result, I know churches inside and out, from memberships of 150 to 2300, in Connecticut, Michigan, Wisconsin, and Pennsylvania. I even preached three times, thus experiencing the pulpit viewpoint.

Like other church families, though, we locked ourselves into the local Sunday morning worship services. Only during summer vacations did we visit other churches. Unfortunately, little inspiration sprouted from those off-season visits except material for an article on "Half-closed Doors."

Since my husband's retirement, however, we have visited a different church almost every Sunday. This has turned into a continual hot and cold pursuit. Sometimes we reach celestial heights. At other times we wonder how worship services can be so dull. But always we contact sincere, dedicated members of the cloth and pew.

Where once upon a time church services followed predictable patterns, now they often surprise. In fact, in our experience, innovations have made Sunday morning worshiping in strange churches vital, renewing, and exciting.

That's why I want to share them with you who loyally attend your local church or are tied to your own pulpit. You can't possibly have the time and flexibility to experience such a worship pursuit.

Thousands of loyal church people, in like circumstances, make up this worship travelogue. I am only the guide — pointing out God's handiwork and his servants' exciting explorations.

1. Music

Of course the Episcopal Church has absolutely gorgeous music. You can't forget it, and if you grew up with it, to leave it is a terrible thing. It's not rational. It's an artistic, fairly unconscious thing.

Quoted by Edward A. Rauff in
Why People Join the Church.

Lay people are tired of reading; they want to sing. People want to rejoice.
If they want to shout, let them shout. Some people are clappers — let them clap.

Charles Whittle

Hallelujah!
Worshipers get emotionally involved even in non-amen, non-charismatic services. Something inherent in human beings responds to rhythm and beat and musical crescendos. However, when they express their feelings as audibly as one conservative congregation did, that's news.

Concluding a triumphant, trumpet-sounding Easter service, the choirs sang Handel's "Hallelujah Chorus."

Emotionally charged by the power and beauty of this great masterpiece, individuals in the congregation spontaneously sang the familiar words, too. Uninhibited by the formal liturgical decorum expected and practiced here, they joined the "endless line of splendor" that had praised God throughout the centuries.

A youthful voice in the balcony shouted: "Hallelujah" after the finale. And the standing congregation applauded. Their ovation thundered as loudly as any Lincoln Center audience's after a grand opera production.

Was not this expression of Easter elation a supreme example of corporate worship, I wondered, as I felt the tug of celestial ecstasy. Later, when I recalled this soul-satisfying service, I remembered what James F. White wrote concerning Christian worship.[1]

"It is something that one can only experience in a living, breathing congregation."

Not only *experienced*, but *expressed*, I might add from the pew viewpoint.

Congregation Sings with Choirs

On two occasions in one church, the congregation has sung part of the anthem with the choirs.

• Once the anthem was the Old Hundredth Psalm Tune by Ralph Vaughn Williams. The choir sang all four stanzas found in hymn twenty-one (United Methodist Hymnal).

The congregation then joined the choirs in singing an additional stanza, printed in the bulletin.

To Father, Son, and Holy Ghost,
The God whom heaven and earth adore,
From men and from the angel host
Be praise and glory evermore.

• The choir director planned the same procedure the Sunday he selected the anthem "Rise, Shine" by Dale Wood. Only this time the musical score, as well as words, appeared in the bulletin, as follows:

---

[1] *Introduction to Christian Worship*, James F. White, Abingdon, 1980, p. 22.

4. Tell how the Fa- ther sent his Son to save us. Tell
of the Son, who life and free- dom gave us. Tell how the
Spir- it calls from ev- 'ry na- tion His new cre- a- tion.

Taped Accompaniment

A small, sophisticated resort chapel boasts no choir. The soloist for the day, however, provided a variety of musical background by tape.

She sang three carols, each originating in a different country. These she introduced by relating their history and explaining that two had pretaped accompaniments.

The first, "What Child Is This?" she sang along with harp and chimes. A cappella mixed voices (including her own) accompanied the second solo. The third, though, she sang with the organist playing "live."

By sharing unseen instrumentalists and singers this way, the soloist expanded musical input in a limited chancel space.

Processional Stops

The choir started processing, then suddenly stopped in their tracks. The lead singers had reached the front row of pews. The others had spaced themselves evenly along the center aisle. From the positions they sang the next three stanzas of "For All the Saints Who from Their Labors Rest."

Then once more they moved forward, in time to sing the final stanza from the choir stalls.

Whatever the reason for this processional variation, proximity to the choir for those extra minutes seemed to stimulate congregational singing.

Introit

The Wesleyan and Sanctuary Choirs sang their choral introit antiphonally from the sides of the sanctuary.

During the prelude, they silently moved single file down the outside aisles. They positioned themselves evenly from front to rear pews, facing each other across the congregation.

After singing "Antiphonal Psalm" by Hal Hopson, the choirs quietly returned to the back of the sanctuary. From there they processed down the center aisle, as was their practice, while singing the first hymn.

Service of Light

Concordia College Choir (from River Forest, Illinois) used a similar formation in a Lutheran service of chants, prayers, psalms, and hymns.

Choir personnel moved down the aisles on either side of the center aisle. However, because they had so many voices, some choristers had to curve the lines around the back of the pews. Thus the choir sang facing each other across and behind the congregation.

When choir members were in place, the congregation stood. The leader walked down the center aisle and lighted a great candle. At that moment he started the chants.

The program fully instructed the congregation with

directions and printed music, like the Psalmody: "the congregation sings the refrain at the beginning and end of the Psalm." (Psalm 141)

The hymn indicated the following voice variety: Congregation will sing first and last stanzas; choir, second; and women's voices in the congregation, third.

Litany instructions included: "At the words '. . . let us pray to the Lord,' the congregation responds: Lord have mercy." Printed notes with words followed.

Throughout this Service of Light, leader, choir, and worshipers alternated chants and spoken Scripture. Listeners became oral participants, upheld by trained voices.

The script required no audience rehearsal. Biblical liturgy dominates in Lutheran churches. Psalms 4 and 141, therefore, they chanted familiarly. They knew Romans 8:31-39 equally as well.

The choir excelled. The rich baritone voice of the leader intoned reverently. Sacred music of the masters, Scripture, professional voice-trainees, and ordinary people united to create a summit religious experience.

Narrator Speaks within the Anthem

Narrator and choir invoked the "Litany of Thanksgiving," by John Ness. The spoken word smoothly synchronized with organ accompaniment. While giving thanks for many things, the arresting young voice raced rhythmically within the bounds of instrumental phrasing. The choirs sang the framework for this extraordinary narrative.

College Choir

The small sanctuary had no room to seat the seventy young people. Therefore, they waited outside in the Florida March sunshine until anthem time.

As they filed in through a side entrance, three buses chortled an accompaniment outside the open door. The Rochester (Minnesota) Community College Choir was on its annual tour. And luckily we happened in at their Longboat Key stop.

Their singing was as exciting as their presence — vibrant and spiritually stimulating. That they were a diversified group from a secular school made their religious impact even more meaningful.

Latin, for a Change

While Roman Catholics switch to the vernacular, a Protestant church reverted to Latin one Sunday.

The soloist sang "Exultate, Julilate" by W. A. Mozart. Fortunately for members of the congregation, the English translation appeared in the bulletin.

And did the people like it? Yes and no. On the way out after the service we overheard these comments:

"I can take the erudite once. But I prefer the practical — words I understand," said one man. His wife agreed, then added: "At least Latin is a novelty in a Protestant church."

Kilted Band Leads Processional

The metropolitan, cathedral-gothic East Liberty Presbyterian Church (Pittsburgh, Pennsylvania) broke all formality to host the Alma College (Michigan) kilted band.

Bag pipes wheezed, as players paraded up and down the two block open mall in front of the church before the service. The band then led the procession up the center aisle of the nave to the choir stalls. They played for congregational singing during the formal liturgy that followed.

Make a Joyful Noice

"It was better than a symphony concert," a visitor commented at the close of a Mother's Day worship service.

A Bach prelude: "Toccata and Fugue in D Minor," an anthem by the Crusaders (children and youth), and another by three combined choirs, crescendoed into the offertory anthem: "A Shout of Sacred Joy."

The Sanctuary Choir (adult) alternately sang and spoke "O for a shout of sacred joy to God, the sov'reign King!" Organist and percussionists (with tambourine, triangle, cymbals and drum) accompanied with enthusiastic sound.

The final shout brought forth an audience echo of "Shout!" And ripples of joyous laughter ran through the crowded sanctuary.

Musical Grace Notes

• Two adult choirs of different denominations exchanged churches for the morning service one Sunday.

• A large church with a magnificent organ and outstanding organist continually provides excellent music. Even with that expectancy, the prelude so inspired the worshipers that they clapped their reaction. The act shattered formal decorum momentarily.

• A United Methodist church featured the borough's junior high band on Christmas Sunday.

• Children or young people usually ring bells. But this time robed adults moved from choir to bells and back again.

The bell-ringers were also regular members of the choir. They played both prelude and offertory, and sang the anthem in between.

• This well attended, middle-sized church has no musical instruments, no choir, no soloists — not even a piano or organ in sight. A layman cued congregational singing with a pitch pipe.

• The hymn, "As Men of Old Their First Fruits Brought" (number 511 in the *Methodist Hymnal*), the congregation sang to the tune of "O Beautiful for Spacious Skies."

• Harp music preceded and followed periods of silence. During the quiet times, worshipers read silently prayers printed in the bulletin. Neither they nor the minister prayed aloud.

• The congregation *sings* the Lord's Prayer every Sunday in a Unity service. It caps the "Thought for the Week," a five-minute meditation period.

One Sunday, for instance, the minister expanded the idea: "I am radiating God's love!" Five times during this thought-development, he asked the congregation to repeat aloud: "I am radiating God's love!" Concluding the final shout, the people burst into song: "Our Father . . ."

• Prayer hymns, hummed by the choir or played softly by the organist accompany this unique introduction to the Lord's Prayer.

Never is this prayer a rider, attached to the pastor's prayer. It stands alone, framed by the music and descriptive, reverent phrases to set the mood. For example, these words the pastor spoke one Sunday:

"In search of a way to express themselves, they asked him how to pray. And he taught them saying: 'Pray then like this . . .' " Worshipers then said the Lord's Prayer.

This musical and narrative preface alerts people to the prayer's intent. They pray with full consciousness of each word. And by changing music and words each Sunday, this prayer-prelude continues to stimulate.

Summer Music

July Camp Meetings

This is not an arm-raising, hand-clapping, foot-stomping church. Quite the opposite. It features acolytes, church year liturgies, and ecclesiastical paraments.

Therefore, a "Camp Meeting" interlude, injected in the middle of the service, was innovative indeed. (The bulletin noted with appreciation the services of a retired minister song leader and a lay pianist during the July camp meetings.)

After the usual candle lighting, versicle, Doxology, invocation, Lord's Prayer, and anthem, these two men took charge. We sang all verses of every song on the bulletin insert sheet. "The Way of the Cross Leads Home." "Love Lifted Me." "Count Your Many Blessings." And finally we sang "Spirit of the Living God" as preparation for the pastoral prayer.

The interlude was a faint facsimile of the old-fashioned camp meeting song-fest. In this formal setting, though, the pianist seemed reluctant to pound out the extra trills and chords characteristic of evangelistic playing. Nonetheless, the congregation sang lustily. And the old gospel songs roused nostalgic feelings.

Men's Chorus

A fifty-voice Summer Men's Chorus sings on Sunday mornings in a mainline church on a Florida Key. While other churches have no choirs during vacation months, this chorus sings en masse.

They observed Father's Day with "Rise Up O Men of God."

Church Family Choir

The summer Family Choir walked down the aisle with all the pomp and dignity of a robed procession. Only these choristers wore sports shirts and summer casuals.

According to the bulletin, this "Summer Family Choir" was having a wonderful experience "sharing and lifting their voices in praise each Sunday." And anyone could join at any time. They rehearsed briefly at 9:15 a.m. for the 10:00 service.

The Sunday we attended this congregational Christian church, whole families of all ages made a joyful contribution of feeling and beauty to our worship.

Sunday Church School Class Fill-in Music

That August Sunday, seven members of the Young Married Couples Class sang religious camp songs. Three others accompanied them on guitars.

During choir vacation months, a different Sunday church school class provided the music.

Father's Day Choir

A choir of grandfathers and fathers sang the hymn-anthem for Father's Day. Anyone in those categories was welcome.

The men met and rehearsed for forty-five minutes immediately before the service. They selected "Faith of Our Fathers."

Barbershoppers Sing

Forty men processed, singing "Onward Christian Soldiers." Their harmony and beat added a new dimension to the familiar hymn. And later, when they sang "Battle Hymn of the Republic," it "raised the hair on your arms" — as the national president of SPEBSQSA says all barbershop music should do when done right.

The Chorus of the Keys of the Society for the Preservation and Encouragement of Barbershop Quartet Singing in America, Inc. presented the special music that August Sunday morning. Two members of the chorus belonged to the church where they were singing, which might account for the men being there.

However, the minister explained that the Chorus of Keys, as part of their community support activities, offers this service. They sing in churches whose choirs are on vacation during the summer months.

The male chorus filled the choir stalls, participated in the liturgy, and sang sacred selections at intervals throughout the ritual: "All Hail the Power of Jesus Name," "Abide with Me," "I Believe," and "The Battle Hymn of the Republic."

Following the service, one of the choristers offered these facts. "This is our sixth service this season, in as many different churches. We love to sing," he said. "And sharing is sheer joy!"

Many of the listeners caught that joy and voiced their appreciation individually to the visitors.

Benediction Responses

• One choir sang two verses of "How Great Thou Art" for their benediction response.

• An associate minister incorporated the Lord's Prayer into her benediction. She recited it interpretatively.

When she concluded: "But deliver us from evil," the choir joined in. They sang the last lines of Malotte's musical version:

"For thine is the kingdom and the power and the glory forever. Amen."

The transition between speaking and singing was less than a breath-pause. Benediction and response were one.

String Quartet

Guest instrumentalists played violins, viola, and cello for prelude, offertory, and postlude. They were participating in New College's annual Summer Musical Festival.

A note in the bulletin suggested: "Those who desire may remain seated for the instrumental postlude. Other worshipers are asked to leave quietly so as not to disturb those who wish to listen."

The majority stayed to hear Beethoven's Third Movement.

Favorite Hymns of the Congregation

Eighty-five people responded when asked to list their ten favorite hymns. The committee compiling results recorded ten points for each hymn in first place, nine points for second place, et cetera. Total tabulations appeared on the Sunday bulletin cover: the ten top favorites, in order of points earned.

The worship service included congregational singing of selected stanzas from each of these top ten. And the ministers alternately introduced each with human interest stories about the hymnists.

Also, the following bulletin captions wove the hymns into the congregation's accepted worship pattern.

A HYMN CALLING US TO PRAISE . . . "Holy, Holy, Holy"

A HYMN CALLING US TO CONFESSION . . . "Rock of Ages"

A HYMN OF GOD'S GRACE . . . "Amazing Grace"

A HYMN OF PRAISE . . . "Blessed Assurance, Jesus Is Mine"

A HYMN OF GOD'S CREATION . . . "This Is My Father's World"

A HYMN OF CONFIDENCE . . . "A Mighty Fortress Is Our God"

A HYMN CALLING US TO PRAYER . . . "What a Friend We Have in Jesus"

A HYMN OF CONSECRATION . . . "Just as I Am" (Sung as the offertory dedication prayer.)

A HYMN OF WITNESS . . . "I Love to Tell the Story"

A HYMN TO LIVE BY . . . "How Great Thou Art"

The senior minister further involved worshipers by asking questions, such as: "Were all ten hymns your personal favorites? were nine of them? Eight . . .?"

Lastly, he asked: "Were none of the ten among your favorites?" Several hands went up.

This diversity of hymn favorites represented the many religious backgrounds of this Southern church's members, the pastor concluded.

At this point, he shared the findings of the personal survey he had made. During the past year, 140 different hymns had filled 172 hymn slots in Sunday morning worship. And only thirty-two times had any of the ten favorites been sung.

While introducing the last hymn, the youth minister said that frequently parishioners asked, "Why don't we sing more old hymns?"

"Paradoxically, though," he continued, "You chose a modern hymn as top favorite. Although adapted from an old Swedish song, 'How Great Thou Art' has been sung in the United States for only thirty years."

Following the benediction, the congregation sang "How Great Thou Art." (Copies of the hymn had been pasted inside the back cover of the hymnal.)

Sing-along

On two gigantic screens, one on either side of the pulpit, flashed the words and musical score of gospel choruses. A small, white spotlight bobbed along, in time to the music — setting the pace, like a baton.

For half an hour, the congregation stood and sang, accompanied by a brass band. Prayers and preaching followed this musical demonstration of joy and testimony.

Rain Inspired Anthem

Timing made this musical experience unusual. It is included here to show how flexibility can contribute to worship excitement.

After a long Florida drought, with fifty grass and brush fires recorded in the county the previous weekend, rains came. To herald this blessing, the choir sang a portion of *Elijah* "as an offering to God on behalf of the congregation."

For weeks, the Sanctuary choir had been rehearsing that section of Mendelssohn's *Elijah* which tells about Elijah's people suffering through a great drought. Elijah pleads with God to send rain: "Open the heavens and send us rain!" Many times he had a youth go forth "to look toward the sea" for signs of rain. Finally, the youth discovers clouds. Rains come, and the people offer a great hymn of thanksgiving: "Thanks be to God. He laveth the thirsty land. The waters gather, they rush alone!"

Originally scheduled for the following Sunday, the choir felt that *now* — immediately after the rains — was the appropriate time to give thanks for relief from the drought. So they switched anthems.

Jazz Band Brings Notes of Joy

As the pastor ended her sermon about the "great cloud of witnesses" mentioned in Hebrews, an improvised Dixieland band played "When the Saints Go Marching In."

To introduce a jazz band into a worship service was the idea of Virginia Hilton, pastor of Albany United Methodist Church (California). "To add input and carry the sermon's message further," she suggested to her husband, Rev. Bruce Hilton. He caught her enthusiasm and organized the "Joyful Noise Jazz Band."

Since that initial appearance, the band has been a part of many worship services. They play jazz spirituals and hymns, such as "The Old Rugged Cross" and "Just a Closer Walk with Thee" — in addition to prelude, offertory, and postlude.

Jazz is not new in church worship, just lost and revived, Mr. Hilton notes. "It was initially played after the Civil War in churches that used band instruments left from the war because they could not afford pianos."

Reported with permission of *United Methodist Reporter*

2. Holy Communion

What did I find of value in the church service? I must admit that the participation of the congregation in the Communion Service was the most moving and eloquent part of the one I attended.

Pierre Burton

Individual and Corporate Interpretation

Twelve white-coated Elders passed the communion elements throughout the congregation. In the meantime, the minister instructed communicants as follows:

"In order that we might recognize God's love for us individually, please eat the bread as you receive it.

"To recognize the corporate body of Christ, please hold your cup of wine until all are served. Then we will drink at the same time."

Extra Bread Distributed

Communicants at Arlington Church, Kensington, California, took home extra elements to share with family and friends.

Stewards prepared plenty of bread. They also provided tiny bottles of wine for this purpose.

However, the clergy later changed this practice. To avoid having teenagers carry bottles of wine, they limited the sharing to bread only.

As another variation, the pastors broke off pieces of bread before communion, as parishioners named persons they felt

needed strengthening. Communicants carried the bread to those
named, after the service.

Families Serve Communion

In this small parish, families take turns making the bread.
On their assigned dates, they also prepare and serve the Lord's
Supper.

Communion within Broadcast Time

The communion service in a radio church was streamlined
smoothly to fit into live broadcast time.

Ten Elders processed to the altar. There they formed a
semicircle on either side, half facing the congregation. After
the minister spoke the words "Take. Eat . . ." one of the Elders
prayed informally. He related the act of taking communion
to the lives and needs of the worshipers. Again, following the
words "Take. Drink . . ." a second Elder prayed.

The ten men and women then walked to their stations
in the aisles and distributed bread and wine almost simultane-
ously. Each communicant held the tray of wine cups while
the next person lifted a cup, drank the wine, and replaced the
empty cup. Serving three hundred people this way took less
than ten minutes.

An extension of this weekly communion followed the corporate worship. Four more Elders served the remaining elem-
ments to absent members in their homes.

Alternate Methods of Serving

To accommodate differing preferences, the minister alter-
nates two methods of serving communion. One time everyone goes to the altar and kneels. The pastors serve. The next
time, ushers serve communicants in the pews.

Church Gardens

Strolling through memorial gardens has become part of the communion ritual for a Florida Key congregation.

The small church has only one aisle. During resort season visitors crowd in tightly. Therefore, lack of space to move freely to and from the altar necessitated this innovation.

Communicants walk down the aisle to the chancel. After receiving the elements, they exit by side doors into the gardens surrounding the church. Leisurely they meander back to the main entrance. There they re-enter the church and return to their pews. Meanwhile, other people are moving to the altar. Thus the garden phase relieves center aisle congestion.

The process flows smoothly — to spacious skies, shady lawns, flowering bushes, and bird songs.

"It's a very special experience," said one visitor, after her initiation into this indoor-outdoor communion service.

Communion Choice

Its membership includes many denominations. The church's roots, however, are Episcopalian, as is its present minister.

To accommodate the varied denominational customs, communicants may drink wine from a common cup or grape juice from individual glasses. The choice is theirs each Sunday.

Before joining the circle of other communicants, a member who prefers grape juice picks up a small, filled vial from the communion table. Later, when the minister serves the common cup of wine, he pauses in front of each grape juice holding parishioner, in turn, and repeats the same words said over the common cup. The ritual proceeds as smoothly as though all were drinking from the chalice.

---

3. Children and Youth

Could it be that our children are sent by God to prick the balloons of our pomposity?

Dennis Benson and Stan Stewart

Worship Includes Children and Youth

"The church cannot live with rituals that divide the generations as if they had nothing in common," writes John Westerhoff in *Learning Through Liturgy.* * "We cannot afford to accept the separation of children, youth, and adults for distinctive rituals. Community is the gift of shared rituals."

Practitioners of this "shared rituals" concept welcome children in the Sunday morning worship service. They recognize and try to creatively channel children's natural liveliness, enthusiasm, spontaneity, and wonder. More specifically, they are integrating cherub choristers, young bell ringers, and child acolytes and banner bearers into traditional all-adult rituals.

Many child-youth-adult unification efforts on Sunday morning are still exploratory, experimental, sometimes almost apologetic, it seems. But gradually adults are allowing time and space for children to share their gifts in Sunday morning worship. And throughout this integration process, children are learning traditional patterns of communal worship.

Among the more innovative ventures I have observed or personally checked are the following examples.

* Seabury Press, 1978, p. 103.

Junior Sermons

Children's sermons in Sunday morning worship have become as infrequent as Sunday evening services. In only a handful out of a hundred churches does the minister gather little children around him for a Bible story or moral illustration. And where Children's Moments still exist, surprising variations spring forth. For examples, note the following:

Layman dresses up

Mr. Bob bounces down the aisle to greet the children at the chancel. His enthusiasm lifts spirits like balloons. Dressed in black tails and red bow tie, he momentarily breaks the formality of the service. But his showmanship also draws attention to eternal truths he tells the kids. They love him, and listen eagerly. As a master story teller, he delights adults too.

Puppet sermon

The popular puppets of Garden City United Methodist Church present the children's sermon every third Sunday. This regular performance is part of the puppet ministry of an integrated troupe of blacks and whites.

Color the Good Shepherd

A Junior Church group of thirty school-age children sat in three front rows. Each child held a religious coloring book and crayons.

The minister told the story of the Good Shepherd for the children's sermon. In conclusion, he said: "In the books you hold are pictures that illustrate the story I have told you. While I am preaching to the adults, you may color those pictures."

The children stayed through the entire service. But they kept themselves occupied by quietly coloring the Good Shepherd and his sheep.

Echo organ demonstrated

The church had recently installed an echo organ in the back of the sanctuary balcony. On the Sunday of the formal dedication, the organist took charge of the children's sermon time.

He explained the various combinations as an assistant played the notes. He even let a child touch a key or two, under careful supervision.

"Why does the music come from the balcony when you play the organ up here?" asked one curious child. And the organist responded as simply as possible.

The entire congregation benefited from this primary explanation of complicated mechanism.

Choose a toy

Although this idea backfired, it is worthy of a second try. At least in another church.

In preparation for the children's sermon, the young assistant minister collected toys that three preschoolers in the group owned and cherished. He was counting on the youngsters' loyalty to teddy bear, doll, and fuzzy duck — no matter how worn or soiled.

When he showed the toys, the children recognized their own instantaneously. "That's mine!" "My dolly!" "Give me my duck!"

Along with the old toys, the minister also brought forth an enormous new panda and asked each of the children to choose. "Which one of the four toys do you want?"

Evidently, from the young minister's actions, he had expected preference for the familiar toys. But no, each child chose the new, big panda.

Nevertheless, the minister continued his thought for the day: that God loves his own. "God loves everyone of us dearly, no matter how old we are or how we look. God loves us, just like you love your own toys, whether old or new. "In the end, the three children left the chancel clutching their old toys possessively. The minister tucked the new panda out of sight. And the congregation gently chuckled in appreciation.

Letter to God Becomes a Prayer

In place of the chldren's sermon, the little ones composed a letter to God. They dictated while the minister wrote down their input.

He started by asking about letters they do write. Such activity seemed limited to grandparents mostly. "Thank you for presents," explained one child.

"How would you like to write a letter to God?" asked the minister. The children nodded approval.

"What shall we say?" asked the pastor.

"Hi, God! How are you?" yelled one child.

"Tell God I can ride my bike all by myself," said an elfish little girl.

"Thank you. Let's say thank you," called out a small lad, teetering on his knees.

And the thank you's flowed freely. "Thank you for Tiger, my cat." "Thank you for my baby sister, but she cries too much."

The minister wrote hurriedly. Then he stopped and asked: "How will we send the letter?"

"On an airplane!" "A space ship!"

"But how will we know he gets it?" the minister asked. A long pause followed. "Shall we pray our letter? God hears our prayers," he said.

And although the prayer idea was the minister's, not the children's, he read the letter as a prayer. He read exactly what the youngsters had composed. No editing. No transitions. This was the children's letter, read to God, with adults listening in.

Children Give to Worship

"We must change the emphasis in worship and the church to ask, not what the church can do for children, but 'What can children do for the church?' "

A church we often attend follows this philosophy. Once a month, church school classes participate in adult worship.

These integrated services appear to be carefully programmed to school the children in worship structure. They learn to hear and understand the Word because hymns, Scripture, and prayers are familiar. Or those selected are on a level with children's comprehension.

In one service, for example, hymns and gospel songs included: "This Is My Father's World," "Kum-Bah-Yah," and "I Would Be True." For the anthem, children's choir and congregation sang "Jesus Loves Me."

For the responding part of worship, the children share their own worship projects. These may be a song, mini-drama, mime, or choral Scripture reading.

At the service cited above, for instance, members of the five-to-seven-year-old class (along with adults) greeted us at the sanctuary entrance as we entered. Eleven-year-olds led the congregation in repeating the Affirmation of Faith and the Lord's Prayer. Another child recited the Twenty-Third Psalm, while other members of his class interpreted it through body motion.

Typically, the minster gives a sermonette, and children leave halfway through the service. But not until individually or collectively they have given something special to corporate worship.

And when they do leave, the children go to prepare a new worship project. This they share a month later.

Boy Liturgists

Twelve-year-old boys assisted in post-Easter services. Garbed in red junior choir robes with white surplices, they read the collects, Scripture, and prayers with dignity. Someone trained these young liturgists thoroughly in proper decorum, understanding of what they read, voice and diction. They moved smoothly and read effectively.

Scouts Share in Worship

On Boy Scout Sunday, the minister asked members of the church-sponsored troup to come to the chancel. They circled around him and answered questions about scouting. The minister used a hand-microphone, sharing it with the boys as they answered.

They spoke their names; recited the Scout laws; told about local projects, camping, badge requirements, and Boy Scout history. The interviewing seemed to be spontaneous, unrehearsed. Enthusiasm abounded during this youthful encounter.

The congregation caught the real meaning, purpose, and effectiveness of the Scouting program. "I'm delighted that our church gives space and financial support to those active, dedicated youngsters," said a solemn-looking old gentleman to the person beside him. He remarked in a voiced whisper we all could hear. Heads nodded agreement.

Children Share Their Handiwork

Another church brings the children back into the same service they left earlier. While the congregation sings the final hymn, children flock in and give whatever they have made during the extended session.

Sometimes they go directly to their parents to share their handiwork. Other times they bring gifts for the entire audience. Whichever, the offerings relate to their sermonette, Scripture lesson, or church calendar.

One Sunday in Advent season, for instance, each child carried a styrofoam star, covered with silver sparkles. They hung these on a bare Christmas tree, which stood near the altar. Their tree-trimming excitement lit up the sanctuary like a thousand candles. Gleefully, they gave their gifts this way, except for one small boy. He kept his star. No way would he part with it.

Parishioners pressed forward after the benediction. They admired the star-studded tree and talked with the children. Thus, adults stamped their approval on children giving in worship. At least that was our impression, as we participated in the excitement.

Children Create Bulletin Designs

Has a child ever designed your church's Sunday morning bulletin?

Children do at Emerald Grove Congregational Church (Wisconsin). There an annual art project involves Sunday school children of all ages. They draw with black felt pens or crayons. And each "artist" signs his or her picture.

A committee evaluates the drawings for biblical message. They select several for printing. However, they may not choose the same "artist" more than once in five years.

An off-set printer enlarges or reduces the original pictures to fit bulletin space. "Now that our church has a plain paper copier," the pastor says, "more children's art work can appear on bulletins, newsletters, and programs."

The example included here appeared on a Christmas Sunday bulletin. Beth Kari Eyster, age eight, is the artist.

Drawing by Beth Kari Eyster, age 8

Children May Move

Not only are churches including ritual elements that appeal to children, they are also allowing children-in-the-pew to move about in order to see better or to go where the action is.

The accepted movement, of course, is the gathering of children within the chancel space for the children's sermon (as previously discussed). The little ones walk, run, and skip down the aisles. They sit cross-legged or on their knees. They talk. They giggle. And most adults approve their anitcs — or at least tolerate them.

The point is these youngsters are free to act like children. They are not expected to be solemn, silent, miniature adults.

• Other congregations project this freedom throughout the morning worship. For example, at the American Protestant Church in Geneva, Switzerland, ushers seat parents near the aisles. Thus their children may move out into the aisles during hymn singing or when they want to see altar activity. This is expected, accepted motion.

• In a Southern Baptist church pretty little children wandered into front pews after the worship service had started. They freely came and went as they pleased.

When the ushers returned the offering plates to the altar, one child dodged among them. She stood on tip-toe to put a coin in the top plate. During the sermon another child quietly walked across the front of the church and put money on the altar.

At least a half dozen youngsters, at one time or another, walked out the door at the right of the pulpit. Moments later they came back through a door on the left. They wandered freely up and down the aisles. They sat with any adult they chose. Then they moved to the front pews again, quietly and gracefully. They did not talk or rattle papers. They just moved.

Definitely, these children felt at home in God's house. And why not? They were free to act as children. In fact, the most heart-warming part of worship that morning we visited was the adult acceptance of children and their interruptions.

Children Sing to Enjoy

Among the varieties of children's choirs, this one is noteworthy for its defined purpose. In the bulletin appeared this explanation: "They join us, not to sing every Sunday, but to sing the songs they enjoy."

However, the very Sunday that notice was printed, the children did sing. Their selections verified what they liked: "I'd Climb the Highest Mountain," "The Impossible Dream," and "Kum-Bah-Yah."

This children's group meets every Wednesday after school. They sing for the fun of it. Consequently, theirs is not a disciplined choir routine. This, of course, limits their appearances. But when they do sing for worship, as they did on that Boy Scout Sunday, their joy and enthusiasm mounts as high as the mountain they sang about.

Adopt a Kid

"Adopt a Kid" was the project launched for a single Sunday in an Eastern parish. Its purpose was to woo more adult approval of children in morning worship, according to the Children's Director.

As adults entered the church, greeters asked if they would like to have a child sit with them during the service. (The youngsters were Sunday church school members who were willing to be adopted. Their parents approved the sharing experience, too.)

A few adults declined the offer. The majority, however, accepted the next child in the line-up. (Choosing specific kids was discouraged, so no one would be left out.)

Reactions to this close proximity to wriggling children varied.

"They don't sit still," observed one adopter.

"I sensed how starchy our adult worship must seem to the boy beside me," said another parishioner.

"A few more encounters like this and in the future we won't have to ask 'where are all the young people?' " one of the deacons pointed out.

The Nativity Story Is Ever New to Children

Children have been the magic force in Christmas Sunday morning worship at a metropolitan cathedral-style church for fifty years or more. The annual nativity pageant has involved thousands of youngsters: Toddler cherubs. Little boy and girl angels with gossamer wings. Big and little boy shepherds with dirty hands and feet, a couple carrying live lambs. Boy lackeys, bearing Magi gifts. Street children darting through the crowds around the busy inn. An adolescent heavenly host.

After processing from various entrances, all converge at the chancel. There a real live baby lies in a manger, attended by a teenage Mary. (One year a donkey stood beside the baby.)

Adults also act in this morality pageant — Joseph, the Wisemen, Gabriel. And without adult direction, choreography, and music there would be no production. Nevertheless, the children make this celebration an extraordinary experience right through the surprise ending.

Young Mary, clutching the real live baby in her arms, runs with Joseph down the center aisle. They flee to save their precious child from the slaughter of the infants. The tremendous bass notes of the mighty organ fill the sanctuary with thunderous crescendo. People scream. Even the children seem to sense the imminent mission of the Christ Child. This dramatic exit turns a "Silent Night, Holy Night" manger scene into a little Good Friday, a harbinger of the Cross.

Twice we have witnessed this magnetic church drama at Calvary Episcopal Church, Pittsburgh, Pennsylvania. It tops all Christmas messages we have ever seen or heard. Costumes, lights, and sound suggest professionalism. But the children give the production the spontaneity and wonder-filled reality of the original nativity in Bethlehem.

Family Lights Advent Candles

Children light Advent candles in several churches, come December. However, families participate in this ceremony in one church.

For example, a father chose and read appropriate scripture for the lighting of the second candle. His kindergarten-age daughter recited a child's prayer poem about candles. The young mother explained the meaning of this symbolic act. And the father helped his toddler son light the candles. The family apparently had created their very own three-minute ceremony.

Informal Nativity Scene Includes All Children

A simple but inclusive Nativity service includes all children on Christmas Sunday. Girls wear homemade angel wings to church. Boys come dressed as shepherds. They sit with their parents as usual.

When the choir starts to sing "Silent Night, Holy Night," that's their cue. They crowd forward to take a peek at the baby Jesus in the manger. Mary and Joseph greet them.

Children who have not come as angels or shepherds may press forward, too. They represent the crowd at Bethlehem.

Carols continue until all have had a look. Then the children return to their seats and formal liturgy follows.

Children Carry Symbols

On Sunday of the Passion, children carried Holy Week symbols to the altar.

The procession included the lighting of the Christ Candle and kindergarteners parading down the center aisle. Each child stopped at the end of an assigned pew. Holding palm branches, they faced inward.

Children carrying the symbols walked between them waving palm branches, up to the altar.

The elements they placed there included: Palms, Chalice and Plate, Rope Whip, Crown of Thorns, Garment of purple, Three Nails, and Cross.

Church School Children Sing and Mime

Church School classes Joy and Joy 3 took part in the worship service the second Sunday in December. (This nondenominational church shares its children with adults once a month.)

For the invocation, the Joy Notes (not labeled as a choir) sang "Away in a Manger." So tiny were they that several did not carry a tune. Their words were distinct, nonetheless.

The Joy Dancers (third graders) mimed "Shepherds Shake Off Your Drowsy Sleep" as a teenager sang this song of praise. (The "dancers" did exactly what we did as children. Only we called interpreting words with movement and gestures *pantomiming*.)

They wore but hints of costumes. A few had leotards and tunics like pages. Some decked Christmas tinsel around their wrists. Several girls swirled in circular skits. They suggested rather than completed their costumes. The effect was the same, however.

Joyettes, a verse choir, spoke the words of "O Come Little Children" for the offertory. The high school soloist then sang the same words.

None of these worship activities reached near perfection. But the children were serious, reverent. And each child contributed toward the ecstasy of Advent.

Youth and Action

"Where have all the young folk gone?" That question often echoes through churches where youths infrequently worship.

For one answer, check out charismatic, non-denominational, independent, and new community congregations. At least in those we have visited, teenagers and young families attend morning services by the hundreds.

Take the Church of the Cross, for example. This eleven year old church's congregation crowds uncomfortably into the sanctuary. The pastor coaxes children to come forward and sit on the floor, to make more pew seats available for adults. Attendance averages a thousand in Sunday morning services. Reportedly, 250 of these are young people; 350, adults; and 400, non-members.

The pastor said that members come from various Christian denominations, "not necessarily because they are disenchanted, but because of the warmth of the church and its freedom of worship." He could also have added that young people come because here is where the *action* is.

"It's like a night club on Sunday morning," commented the person in the pew beside us.

A ten-piece band blasted gospel songs over the amplifiers. The over-crowded sanctuary vibrated with the beat. People clapped, hummed, whistled, sang, and talked throughout these preliminaries. Sixty teenagers sauntered down the aisles and filled the choir space. A junior high choir, which later sang an anthem, sat in front rows.

Ritual had no part in the service. Music, though, played a vital role. In fact, we stood and sang for the first half hour. With organ, piano, and band accompaniment, choirs and congregation sang modern Christian songs, Bible verses set to music, and camp-like choruses. On two huge, white screens, the lyrics flashed in "sing-along-with-Mitch" fashion.

People clapped frequently. They even clapped while the preacher prayed. He asked God to drive the devil from their church, and hundreds clapped so loudly that the minister has to shout the next petition above the din.

Three parishioners, at different times, spoke in tongues. When they did, everyone else became silent. Although not an unsual phenomenon in this church, still it seemed to be unsettling. Children and teenagers watched and listened, as if trying to make out a secret code.

However, young people certainly had no problem understanding the sermon. The preacher spoke their language: vivid, arresting, pictorial. He punctuated biblical episodes with slang, idioms, and the vernacular of the 80s. He spoke with humor, too.

In addition to *being where the action is, young people were also part of the action.* Youths ministered.

They manned the parking lots. A couple dozen high schoolers (including girls) directed traffic, helped mothers with small children, and assisted the handicapped.

Young people greeted visitors at the church door.

Others ushered within the sanctuary. More sat with their families or peers. They played in the band and sang in the choirs.

Where have all the young people gone? Have you visited a newly organized, untraditional church in your community recently?

Preview Offered in Worship Service

The Godspell (RSG) Youth Ensemble sprang from the front pews. Informally, they sat and stood outside the chancel. From there they told about their forthcoming production, to be presented at the next church fellowship supper.

These costumed teenagers sang their own version of "All God's Gifts," a song from the Broadway musical, *Godspell*. They called their abridgement RSG (Revised Standard Godspell).

Following the song and informal chatter, the pastor preached his communion sermon. A surprise contrast it seemed momentarily.

But later, when we took communion, we recalled having received bread and wine on stage between acts of the original *Godspell*. Remembering the extraordinary experience helped us relate this youth version to formal communion.

Sacred Movement

A blithe young woman stepped forward to chancel center. She wore a flowing white nylon robe over a black cassock. While a tenor sang "The Lord's Prayer" by Malotte, she shared her own understanding of the meditation through hand and body actions. (The bulletin defined her interpretation as *Sacred Movement*.)

This act of worship surprised and pleased the conservative congregation surrounding us. They reacted as though this were a "first" in their experience. Grace, youth, and professionalism had added a new dimension to a favorite song.

At the same time, I recalled. For hadn't I moved similarly while pantomiming "O Zion Haste"? That had been years and years ago, at a Sunday evening service in my father's church in Michigan.

Call *Sacred Movement* innovative or renovative. Either way, it can be a spiritual "high" for performer and observer alike.

Sacred Dancers

The choir sang their anthem as usual. But this time youthful, sacred dancers floated down the aisles, rhythmically interpreting the anthem lyrics. In their soft, long pastel tunics, they enhanced the music with color and motion.

Directed by the minister's wife, this teenage group of girls initially danced barefoot in the park at outdoor summer morning worship.

Talking Choirs

Talking choruses are as old as Greek tragedies and as new as talking-people television commercials. In between times, they have been religious too.

A quarter century ago, talking choirs highlighted the World Council of Churches' "Festival of Lights" at Soldiers Field in Chicago. However, in spite of thousands of people participating in this medium, choral speakers remain a novelty in Sunday morning worship. We have heard two during the eleven o'clock hour. Both times young people performed articulately.

• In place of the anthem, three children's choirs of various age groups recited "The Great Guest Comes," a poem by Edwin Markham. Each choir spoke from a different balcony (one on either side of the nave; one in the rear).

Together, they all repeated the first eight lines in unison. For the remainder of the poem, the choirs took turns telling the story. The director had made no effort to divide voices according to pitch and resonance. The age differences among the three choirs provided a natural variation. And probably because the children had had previous musical training, they spoke clearly and followed directions well.

• In another church, a high school reading choir spoke from the chancel area. They recited the twenty-fourth Psalm, the Old Testament reading for the day. The director, a professional in speech, apparently had tested each voice for tone balance.

I conversed with the director after the service, telling her how much I admired the speaking choir's precision and understanding of the Psalm. In response, she shared these observations:

"The kids memorize whole chapters of the Bible. Collects and prayers too. Sometimes we are *group liturgists*.

"These teenagers get first-hand experience in corporate worship. Most of them don't sing well enough to belong to musical choirs. This way, though, they aren't left out of peer participation in the most important church event of the week — Sunday morning worship."

Audio/Visuals Run by Teens

Four teenagers and one adult sat in the brand new electronics booth, prominently projected from the back wall of the nave.

"Up-to-the-minute sound equipment was installed this week," proclaimed the pastor, enthusiastically. "Now we will be rid of the dead spots that have plagued the congregation for years. An electronics media specialist is here to operate and adjust the equipment until all problems are corrected. He is also training a crew to be in charge."

After the service, we examined audio panels and talked with one of the crew members. He projected the pastor's enthusiasm into the future. "The audio can cover expanded space if we have to push the walls out to accommodate new members," he boasted.

Another youth had just finished video-taping the service. "We will show it to shut-ins," he explained.

Teenage Artist Illustrates Sermon Subject

"For the series of sermons, 'Open My Eyes,' various members of the congregation will be helping us to see." This explanation appeared in the bulletin.

The Sunday morning we attended, a photographic study entitled "Sunburst" stood on an easel in the narthex. It was a silk oak in the backyard of the home of the teenager who photographed and enlarged it.

"Frank had the eyes to see something of the glory of God's sun shining through," the minister pointed out in his sermon.

The young man stood beside the picture after the service. "Yes, I am the photographer," he admitted proudly, as people admired his work.

Thus a teenager contributed to the worship experience of many. In return, he received recognition and encouragement. In fact, one parishioner was so impressed with the professionalism of the boy's work that he offered to buy the photograph.

Young Men Preside

• A handsome youth, in Boy Scout uniform, was liturgist. Later in the service, the minister and Scout master gave him the God and Country Award.

• Pre-seminary students added youthful zest to the ritual the Sunday they assisted in the worship service.

Teenagers Talk

This congregation *listened* to teenagers talking about vital international, political issues — controversial ones that raise blood pressure.

"Christian Citizenship" was the worship theme that Fourth of July Sunday. And the young people had just returned from the annual high school Washington seminar. Their enthusiasm grabbed the nappers as they informed and frankly stated their views.

The subjects? El Salvador. Hand gun control. Abortion.

At the same service, a young people's quartet sang a medley of patriotic songs. Also four Boy Scouts led the Pledges of allegiance to the Christian and American flags.

How many other churches have had the courage to let teenagers speak out about their *feelings* concerning national issues, in a morning worship service? Watered down reports of trips and conferences, yes. Student Sundays, planned with national program aids, yes. But kids telling it straight as they see, hear, and understand political problems? Here is a minister who gives up his pulpit and sermon time once a year to informed, inspired youth. And the people *listen!*

---

4. Visuals

In many churches, parishioners are creating their own art for specific liturgical occasions and commemorative events.

Pastors today should be equipped to encourage these modes of expression and to make use of the resources which the artistic world can supply.

Henry Luce III.

My art [designing vestments and banners] springs from my Bible study. I feel a calling to do visual preaching and to do it as a lay woman.

Elaine Wilson
Reported by permission of *United Methodist Reporter*

Outside Message Wins Worshipers
This church rises high on a hill overlooking Parkway East. The congregation has capitalized on the strategic setting for the benefit of all who pass by.

At night, exquisite stained-glass windows glow from inside lighting. On the outside, a message beams brightly along the gables. In Advent season, it reads: *"Glory to God!"* The remainder of the year, it reads: *"Jesus Is Alive!"* Nothing is garish about the display. It appeals, persuades. Snail-paced commuters, traveling bumper-to-bumper along the parkway at dusk, catch the message.

After several months of passing this citadel on the hill, we spent an hour one Saturday afternoon trying to find how to get to it. The next morning, we attended a refreshing, motivating, Episcopal family service.

While there, we learned that many new members had initially come because of the message beamed to them while traveling the parkway.

Marker Entreats Entrance

This Is the Oldest Drive-in Church boasts a sign in front of Whitfield Estates Presbyterian Church.

Although the building itself provoked no second look, nor could we see a vast parking area from the highway, our curiosity caused us to turn in one Sunday morning.

Only a half-dozen motorists parked around us. And when an usher said we had a choice, we moved inside the church, away from the torrid summer heat. Why should we sit outside, while minister and choir performed inside behind glass door partitions in air-conditioned luxury, we reasoned.

The high cement platform projecting in front of the glass doors and the imposing steps leading to it indicated the splendor of past drive-in services. Today only a few worshipers remain in their cars. The main congregation worships within the church — on either side of the minister and choir. The arrangement is unique — two inside transepts full of people, with the imaginary nave being the outside congregation.

The photograph on the bulletin cover shows hundreds of cars parked in symetrical rows like pews, an anachronism for today. Nevertheless, we discovered that a foremost concern here is serving tourists and transients. The friendly, sincere ambience has drawn us back several times.

The drive-in church idea lost its initial impact along with the advent of air-conditioning and acceptance of casual attire in formal services. To meet this change, the original drive-in church offers a combined indoor-outdoor worship.

The only visual contact the indoor congregation has with the outdoor is the offering. Briefly opening the glass partitions, ushers bring the motorists' tithes and gifts.

The outside audience sees the minister and choir through glass, both summer and winter. They hear the service through individual headphones. And they are courteously served by caring ushers.

Architecture Speaks to Worshipers

The modern edifice alerts the passerby to take a second look. From a four-wall concrete square rises a steep pyramid-style roof. And at the pinnacle an aluminum cross pierces the sky. Sabel palms and St. Augustine grass cover the acreage surrounding the church. Altogether, there's something about its functional, friendly, up-to-the-minute architecture that woos. It's for real. It's earthy, yet spiritually oriented. That's why we, along with many other visitors, were magnetically drawn inside — to attend services.

The venture would have been disappointing except for two permanent visual worship symbols — cross and altar. The half-circle sanctuary of wood paneling depended on artificial light. Only slits of ordinary glass panes showed under the projecting eaves. As expected, the ceiling was like a tent, minus a center pole. However, the plain walls and pews accentuated the dramatic white altar. Placed below the apex of the roof, this enormous, floodlighted altar was the focal point of our worship.

Above the altar hung an unusual cross, bearing a fully clothed figure of Christ. No wounds showed. No crown of thorns. No signs of suffering. The face of the Christ-figure was serene.

Only clear-glass entrance and exit doors linked the outside world to the vertical, spiritual sentiments within. Shut out were the chaos of crowded beaches and noise of boat liveries that surround Gloria Dei Lutheran Church.

Walk-through Sculpture

Worshipers walk through a monumental sculpture on their way into First Presbyterian Church of Sarasota, Florida.

Its basic form is a large cross of outlined space, symbolizing Jesus Christ, the Way. As you enter, it is the Way into the church, the Way to God. As you leave, it becomes the Way back into the world that "God so loved." The red brick path you walk suggests Jesus' blood, which was shed for us.

The huge arms of this cross curve slightly upward, as if reaching out to embrace us. And the cross outline opens to the sky at the top, relating Jesus to his Heavenly Father. ("No one comes to the Father except through me.")

Two lesser crosses supposedly intimate our choices: to follow or not to follow Jesus. They are the two thieves' crosses.

One represents the thief who mocked Jesus. It stands alone. Isolated from the Christ-cross, this solid, heavy, block-like structure is grounded in the earth.

The other outlines space like the Christ-cross. Sheltered under an arm of the big cross, one arm of this smaller space-cross opens into the Christ symbol. This portrays the thief's trust in Jesus, his pleas for mercy. Just as Christ is no longer flesh, but Spirit, likewise, the forgiven thief has become one in the Spirit with Him.

The pedestal is shaped like butterfly wings — an ancient symbol of resurrection.

Before visiting this memorial to a former church Elder, I saw the sculptor's model in his Siesta Key studio. At that time, I heard the symbolism explained. So unique was my experience there that I had to see the sculpture itself. That's why we later attended services at First Presbyterian.

The family of William Arthur Shannon, M.D., commissioned Thornton Utz, artist and fellow elder, to create a memorial sculpture, which would proclaim Christ as the Way, the Truth, and the Life. The result is this sermon in stone. It joins the memory of a beloved physician with the creative genius of a church member artist.

After services, we stopped to study the sculpture. On the solid cross stood a young boy. He jumped off, then climbed up again. Momentarily, I thought his actions sacrilegious. But the brochure I had picked up inside the church changed my point of view. One of the purposes for this type of monument, it stated, was that it be a place "where children may play uninhibited." No wonder the child enjoyed his jumping from the cross!

Going and coming through this sculptured space perhaps has become routine for some parishioners. (It was dedicated in 1978.) But as long as the monument stands, its message will excite visitors like us, who pass through it.

"I am the Way, the Truth, and the Life," Christ says again through a modern sculptor's mind and hands.

Sculpture concept copyrighted by Thorton Utz, artist. Used with his permission.

Visual Arts in Worship

A new emphasis on the visual components of worship challenges member artists and handicrafters to contribute their talents. Creativity explodes in churches that favor the arts. Octogenarians crochet altar cloths. Children block print banners. Their mothers quilt choir stoles. Teenagers silk-screen bulletin covers. Woodworkers carve pulpit furniture. Even professional designers sew vestments by hand, using brilliant colors and varied textures.

The following examples excite us:

• A large quilted banner — in successive stages of completion — hung in the sanctuary each Advent Sunday. Guild members quilted another point of the star pattern weekly. The completed star graced the Christmas Eve service.

• An artist member of a California church designed four large banners featuring the Gospels. They covered a bare wall opposite a series of stained glass windows. She edged the banners with the same border designed in the stained glass.

• A professional planned the stained glass windows for a Houston sanctuary. Church members, however, did the actual construction.

• As the assistant minister greeted us after the service, I asked: "May I touch your stole? Its texture fascinates me."

Stitched in needlepoint on a background of liturgical green were Early Church symbols. Fish, boat, and cross blended in muted colors.

The reversible stole felt heavy, coarse, woolly. The handiwork appeared perfect.

"A friend made it for me," the young clergyman explained. "I'm pleased you noticed it."

• Another minister needlepoints his own stoles. He has one for each season on the church calendar.

• Stained-glass windows in a Mexico, Missouri, church inspired the designs for sixteen needlepoint kneelers in a St. Augustine, Florida, church.

The printed legend pressed into my hand as I entered the church revealed these further facts:

— Six women had stitched four miles of two-ply, 100% yarn.

— Each kneeler took about a year from design to completion.

— The yarn alone cost well over $1000.

— If you consider labor costs at minimum wages, the value increases to $5,840. Skilled labor and artistic quality, of course, bring costs well above minimum wage scales.

— The kneelers are insured for $12,000.

• A needlepoint carpet covered the chancel steps to the altar. Christian symbols blazed against a pure white background. The flaming torch sign of United Methodism predominated.

Two needlepoint kneeling pads also extended the full length of the altar railing. Each accommodates twenty communicants. These cushions bore vine and grape symbols, needled on a rich dark brown background.

After several inquiries, we discovered that two long-time members (sisters) had done all the needlepoint. A friend of theirs made the patterns, borrowing freely from traditional Christian symbols.

The artistry reminded us of medieval, old world tapestries. The total impression, though, was fresh, clean, and bright. The artisans carefully had coordinated colors with the sanctuary's rich blue carpeting, warm brown woodwork, and dramatic stained glass windows.

Not all churches buy altars by the foot and crosses by the yard from a catalog. Local woodworkers turn out worship furnishings, too.

• A retired carpenter hand carved two pulpit chairs and a communion table. These he gave to his church, to replace turn-of-the-century furniture. The wood matched altar railings and pews precisely. The workmanship looked flawless.

• While serving in the Armed Forces overseas, a young volunteer fashioned two candlesticks and a cross out of a discarded, broken propeller. These he gave to his chaplain, who used them for chapel communion services.

• A class of teenagers wove the reed baskets that hold the offering in their church services.

• Easter morning an adult choir initiated new crimson robes. They matched perfectly Jesus' red robe in the Gethsemane-scene rose window above the choir loft.

Altar Guild members had embroidered the white stoles worn with the robes.

• *"This Church Can Do Anything It Wants To!"* That message blazed in lights at the top of an electric sign, four-by-eight feet. It stood at the right of the pulpit.

Below the caption, complete with staff and signature, glowed red bulb musical notes and the words: "Send out the light." Definitely, an electronics enthusiast sparked this good-news production.

Baptismal Symbol

The parents received a small towel at the close of their child's christening service. While presenting it, the minister explained: "This linen square came from an old communion table cloth. A shell — symbol of baptism — is embroidered in the center. Perhaps some day, when your child is older, you will give it to her, as an outward sign of her baptism. Members of the Altar Guild make these, to be given at all infant baptisms."

Easter Banners Initiated

Acolytes carried two new Easter banners in the procession. Following the flag-bearers, they placed the banners against the walls on either side of the chancel. So displayed, the congregation could read the message clearly. The one at their left bore the words: *The Lord Is Risen!* The one on their right reaffirmed the tidings: *The Lord Is Risen Indeed!*

Heavy textured white material made up the banners themselves. Black letters, appliqued on the white background, shouted the good news.

The church member who made these beautiful banner gifts also sewed on other Easter symbols. In gold thread, she had embroidered lilies at the bottom of each. And in the upper right hand corner was a crown on one, a cross on the other.

Placed alongside the flags, as they were, these hand-made emblems accented the real meaning of Easter.

Symbolic Candlesticks

Two new altar candlesticks replaced a long-used candelabra. In dedicating these new altar accessories, a member of the worship committee read the following explanation. It also appeared in the bulletin.

"The two candlesticks are the traditional symbols found on Protestant altars and symbolize both the divine and human nature of Christ, our Lord.

"When lighted they express the reality of the words of the Lord, 'I am the light of the world.' As we dedicate these symbols relfecting simple dignity and majestic grace, let us offer the prayer, 'Lord, accept these memorials to your Glory from grateful hearts.' Amen."

• Following the ritual for receiving new members during the worship service, each single or couple received a gift. It was a commemorative plate, picturing the church.

Circle Symbolism

During the energy crunch, one congregation moved from the cavernous sanctuary into an all-purpose room for morning worship. The parishioners sat in a theater-in-the-round arrangement.

"This seating plan," explained the minister, "symbolizes the unbroken circle of Christian fellowship."

In the center, cross and chalice stood on a velvet-draped table. The minister moved about this focal point. He kept contact with everyone in the circle by turning around from time to time. Two lay persons, who prayed and read the Scripture, did likewise.

Symbolic Colors

Bolts of bold, bright cotton cascaded from the balconies that surrounded the small sanctuary. The effect was breathtaking: sunshine gold, cardinal red, royal blue. However described, the loosely flung banners proclaimed liturgical colors.

The edifice was of "Little Brown Church in the Vale" vintage. Worship patterns and preaching were traditional, which added to the color surprise.

After the service, we asked questions and met the color coordinator. She led us to the balcony to show us how the banners were thumb-tacked under the railing.

"Color talks," the lady said. "And our church is so drab. We can't afford a dorsal drapery or stained glass windows. But we can afford mill-ends of fabric. Pieces of colored cloth can symbolize joy, adoration, love, and sacrifice just as well as more expensive items, can't they?"

The celebration colors had already proved her point.

Pentecost Red

On Pentecost Sunday, the altar blazed with red gladioli and tall tapers. Ministers and choir members wore crimson stoles over white robes.

The color red dominated throughout the congregation, too. Alerted by newsletters, many members donned red clothing or accessories. White-haired women wore red dresses; ushers, red jackets or coats; junior church children, red ribbons and ties.

The symbolic, personal involvement made this particular Pentecost memorable. The worship service itself pointed up the religious calendar significance of the day.

Horn of Plenty

On the altar, a mountain of fresh fruits and vegetables

spilled out of a gigantic cornucopia. Green onions, carrots, artichokes, red cabbage, celery, egg plant. Bananas, apples, oranges, avocados, grapes. Together they symbolized God's plentiful supply and our Thanksgiving Day.

No one called attention to the cornucopia during the service. After the benediction, though, parishioners flocked forward to get a close-up view.

Our personal thanks went to the Great Creator. However, we would have liked to personally thank the artist who put together this masterpiece. We shall see it in our mind's eye forever.

Paschal Candle Lit

An enormous white candle, placed in an equally over-sized brass candlestick, stood beside the pulpit. The acolyte lit it before he lit the altar candles.

Members of the congregation who had not seen the initial lighting of the big candle at the first service on Easter wondered about it. This particular United Methodist church had never before used the Paschal Candle.

The uninformed soon learned, however, that this has been an historic church symbol. The candle varies in size. For instance, in the Middle Ages, one reportedly weighed three hundred pounds.

They also learned that their big candle symbolized *Christ's risen presence on earth*. Therefore, the acolyte would light it at every worship service until he put it out on the Day of Pentecost.

Tongues of Fire

A Protestant church revived an old Italian symbolic act. From side and back balconies, parishioners scattered red and yellow and orange flower petals. These drifted down onto the heads of the congregation below. The petals supposedly simulated the tongues of fire. The enactment, of course, took place on Pentecost Sunday.

Symbolic Nails

The white styrofoam cross held special meaning for individual members of the congregation on Easter morning. Lilies and garlands of green covered the nail holes. But they knew the holes were there.

On Ash Wednesday, parishioners of this Catholic church had opportunity to take a nail from this cross, to keep as a symbol of something each wanted to give up or overcome during Lent. On Good Friday, nail-keepers put them back into the cross *if* they felt they had carried through their intent. (Some did. Some did not. And, of course, not all parishioners at either service participated.)

Easter morning the nails no longer pierced the cross. They had been removed. The empty cross thus symbolized triumph and new beginnings.

In relating to me her involvement, one participant told this story. Her beloved mother had died. The daughter had grieved for five months. Her sorrow was soul-consuming. She knew she had to break free of it.

The nail from the cross became her incentive. It tied Christ's suffering with her own. After much prayer and intrapersonal struggle, she was ready to replace the nail in the cross on Good Friday.

"On Easter morning," she said, "I felt as though a great burden had left me. The white cross symbolized my victory over grief."

Symbolic Mood

A lack of things communicated a somber mood during a Fifth Sunday in Lent worship service.

The altar held no flowers. The candles remained unlighted. Only the plain gold cross looked familiar.

From side doors, the choir moved like shadows into the loft. Their low-key entrance contrasted radically with their usual ceremonial processional down the center aisle. No crucifer, no flag and banner bearers preceded them. They wore plain black robes, minus stoles.

Lights dimmed during the anthem: "Lighten Our Darkness" by Robert Leaf. "O Lord, have mercy, lighten our darkness. We've all been temptors; we've all been traitors; we've all denied you. Our light is black."

Because of this stripping of joyous symbols and sound, a feeling of impending tragedy enveloped us. And the minister further projected this sensation into his sermon. He spoke from the text: "When the chief priests and officers saw him, they cried out saying, 'Crucify him, crucify him.' "

Even the reds and golds of stained glass windows glowed dimly. For outside sullen clouds hid the sun. Only the subdued, indirect lights of the horizontal cross gleamed faintly above the worshipers.

For the closing hymn, we sang: "Beneath the Cross of Jesus, I fain would take my stand." Could any other hymn be more meaningful in that symbolic service? We were literally standing beneath the cross.

Symbolic Gestures

Arms stretch upwards. Feet tap out the rhythm. Bodies sway to and fro. The chorus crescendos. A man beats the wall with his fists as he talks in tongues. Divinely inspired bodily action possesses these charismatic worshipers.

At a tabernacle worship service, white-robed teenagers (with tinsel halos atop their flowing hair) float down the center aisle. They pantomime their way to the cross that stands on the high platform. "I am coming to the cross. I am poor and weak and blind." While the chorister leads the huge crowd in song, the young ladies lithely glide forward. Toes point. Arms reach outward. They skip. They hesitate. They are dramatizing their inner feelings about the hymn's message and music.

Called by whatever name, the charismatic motions and tabernacle pantomimes involve the same basic bodily actions as those used by the Yale Liturgical Dancers. Gestures show *feeling, emotion.*

For instance, the Yale Divinity group interprets how Moses felt at the edge of the Red Sea. He had led the Children of Israel out of captivity. He holds out his staff. The Red Sea parts. The dancers reach, turn, kneel, leap, to interpret their inner reactions to the biblical story.

The dancers explain (when they feel it necessary) that they are doing nothing new. Dance is part of our Judeo-Christian heritage. Examples from the Bible are many. "David *danced* before the Lord with all his might." 2 Samuel 6:14

Miriam, the Prophetess, at the Red Sea led Israelite women in a *dance* to celebrate God's intervention and their freedom from bondage. (Exodus 15:20) And Jesus, in telling the Prodigal Son story, referred to music and *dancing* at the celebration of the Lost Son's return home.

Traditionally, worship had been made up of symbolic gestures associated with the dance. Therefore, the only novelty in liturgical dancing today is that groups who practice it *call* themselves *dancers.* Unlike secular dancers, though, they worship God in their dance. They communicate through motion rather than words.

Yale Liturgical Dancers have participated in worship services throughout the New Haven, Connecticut, area. Among their dance interpretations have been an Israeli candle dance to welcome the Sabbath, and a betrothal celebration, based on Colossians 3:12-17.

Founder's Day Ceremonies

In her syndicated column, Ann Landers printed a letter from a reader who complained about Protestant worship services. He felt they were too social, too frivolous, too far from serious worship.

For a follow-up, Landers printed a dozen responses from all over the United States. Among them was a letter written by the oldest member of a church in Hyattsville, Maryland. She wrote: "The day you printed the West Coast letter, the entire congregation sang 'Happy Birthday' to me. I loved it!"

I recalled this column when the woman who is the oldest living resident of Sarasota, Florida, as well as the oldest member of First United Methodist Church, was honored at a Founder's Day worship service. A relative wheeled her down the aisle to the chancel. There, a child gave her a white frosted cake with four lighted pink candles. (The four candles represented the number of years she has lived beyond the hundred mark.) The thousand or more worshipers and choir sang "Happy Birthday." And the Oldest Member smiled her thanks.

Too social? Too frivolous? It's all in your point of view. We were impressed by the love displayed with dignity, within a formal service.

The birthday cake and candles were among several visual expressions of Founder's Day. The stained glass windows also played important roles.

The associate pastor first drew our attention to the window above the choir. Among the symbols in stained glass, he pointed out the globe and the script, *Go Into All the World and Preach the Gospel*. "This is our commission," he said.

The pastor singled out four other windows. Before each in turn, he stood and told the biblical story pictured in glass. A teenager explained the meaning of the symbols. And a layman at the lectern gave a brief biography of the donor. He also read the names of descendants, family members of the doner who sat in pews nearest to their ancestor's window.

As they heard their names, these honored guests moved toward the window. There a professional photographer snapped a group picture. In the meantime, the pastor moved on to another window.

The descendants present numbered as many as thirty per window. From a babe-in-arms through four generations, these guests became a visual link to the founders of the local church.

An Explosive 4th of July Sunday Morning Worship

The Church of the Nazarene quarter-page advertisement on the Saturday church page of the local paper piqued our curiosity. Why not celebrate the 4th at their eleven o'clock service, as the ad encouraged readers to do? What we experienced was a nerve-tingling, tear-teasing God and Country service, exploding with symbols. The professional quality of the visual aids, the timing and finesse of their displays were extraordinary. And the people-participation was devout.

Foyer decorations preluded the continual unfurling of flags throughout the service. Even before we entered the church, small American flags had marked our passage from parking lot to church doors.

Inside, opposite the main entrance, were huge white blocks, piled like children's toys. Stars and poster prints of Washington and Lincoln covered the block sides. From this patriotic presidential display, banners covered the walls the length of the foyer. Red and white stripes alternated with white-starred blue banners, symmetrically arranged.

A large white cross was the focal point within the sanctuary. It hung flat against the dorsal wall, above choir and pulpit. On either side of the cross, an oversized flag stretched flat against the paneled wall. And high above these three symbols hung twenty banners, like the stars and stripes in the foyer.

Red and white carnations covered the altar table. And to complete the patriotic decor, tens of miniature flags danced among palm trees on both sides of the front pews. (Electric fans kept them activated.) All flags were American except the Christian flag, placed beside the pulpit.

The symmetry of design and placement of flags and banners seemed to symbolize order — with the cross the focal point.

Decorations, though, were only part of a completely symbolic service, which proceeded in the following order:

• A fifty-voice choir and large orchestra opened the worship with a rousing, glass-shattering musical tribute, "This Is My Country."

• A ninety-three-year-old veteran of World War I read the invocation.

• Eight color guards ceremoniously marched down the aisles and placed large flags on either side of the nave. The color guards, dressed in various uniforms, represented both armed and community services: Army, Navy, Air Force, Marines, Coast Guard, Police, Firemen, and Eagle Scouts.

• Everyone in the congregation who had served in the Armed Forces or are serving at the present time stood for plaudits. Also recognized were those present who had lost loved ones while serving our Country. (This Memorial Day and Armistice Day procedure seemed especially appropriate on Independence Day.)

A commissioner represented county government. She spoke briefly, emphasizing the importance of a single vote.

The pastor challenged us to accept the Christian's responsibility to participate in government, as well as to vote.

The pageantry of the flags climaxed with the singing of "The Battle Hymn of the Republic." The congregation joined the choir in singing the last stanza. And timed with the added volume, an enormous flag (35'x50') slowly crept up the dorsal wall. It was fully exposed when "Glory, glory, Hallelujah! broke the decibel level expectancy. That sound and sight worship finale grabbed our emotions and held them suspended throughout the benediction.

Friendship Sunday

"Catch the Spirit" was the theme of *Friendship Sunday* at Trinity United Methodist Church. And indeed, the congregation *did* "catch the spirit" with the aid of multiple visuals.

• As people entered the sanctuary on that early June morning, they walked down an aisle lined on either side by beribboned bouquets of roses: a basket at the end of each pew. These bright floral arrangements and the mass of flowers on the altar were given by friends to honor friends. (Thirty-four givers' names appeared in the bulletin.)

• Leading the procession, eight bearers of enormous, easy-to-read, handcrafted banners preceded the choir. These symbols of friendship remained throughout the service, erectly placed in pots of sand at the front of the sanctuary. Members of various Sunday church school classes carried them — adults, teenagers, and children. Each banner was a class project. And two special banners spelled out "Catch the Spirit! and "Share the Spirit."

• Business-size cards, inserted in the bulletin, bore the printed caption: *Celebration of Friendship.* Three lines spaces were beneath the words: *Friends to pray for.* Worshipers placed these small cards on the altar during prayer time.

• First-time visitors stood during the welcome period, and ushers wrote down their names and addresses — so that fresh, hot pies could be delivered to them in their homes after the services. (This is a once-a-year friendship act.)

• The visual climax of this Celebration of Friendship on Pentecost Sunday was the ascension of hundreds of red balloons.

The pastor gave the benediction on the lawn, before we released our "Catch the Spirit" balloons. The congregation sang the recessional hymn as they followed the choir out of the church. (Copies of "God of Grace and God of Glory" were in our bulletins, so we could leave our hymnals in the pews.) We continued singing until everyone held a balloon.

After the benediction, the choir and congregation sang the response: "Joy to the World." On the cue of the "amen" we let go our balloons. The brisk breeze carried them high and far. Only one remained hanging in a nearby tree.

• Strangers intimately talked with strangers as they walked into Fellowship Hall to the *Reception for Friends*. And later, in time for dinner dessert, many received friendly short visits and hot homemade pies in their own homes.

Ten Little Apples

As the layman approached the lectern, he turned abruptly, retraced his steps to the front pew, picked up a brown paper bag, and returned to the lectern. His commission that Sunday morning preceding the annual financial drive was to activate giving during the next three minutes.

First he suggested that we imagine that Jesus is standing in the pulpit, speaking to us, sharing our needs and concerns about everyday living. "Imagine Jesus relating this parable."

"All of you have certain financial needs and preferences to meet. For example, *food*." At this point, the layman reached in the bag and pulled out an apple. "This apple stands for that part of your income that goes for food," he explained, as he laid the red apple on a stand beside him.

Again he reached into the bag and pulled out an apple. "This symbolizes that part of your money which you spend for housing." Again and again, he dipped into the paper bag for another apple. These he placed alongside the first two. They represented that portion spent on clothing, health, taxes, savings, education, recreation and hobbies, transportation and travel.

Nine apples sat in a row. The tenth, however, he held high. "Are you giving this portion of your money to me? A tenth of your income. A *tithe*?"

He paused. Then he cut a piece out of the apple and held it toward us. "Or are you giving me a *gift*?"

He paused once more, then sliced a silver of apple from the piece. Barely visible, so tiny it was. He held it on the end of the knife. "Or are you giving me a *tip?*"

The congregation remained stone-deaf quiet as the layman picked up the apples, the pieces and the paring, stuffed them back into the paper bag, and returned to his front pew seat.

---

5. Church Outreach

The Christian community's worship is an extension of its service, and its service is an extension of its worship.

Douglas Hall*

Bulletins Aid Worshipers

Bulletins serve important purposes. They prepare worshipers for the service. They ease participation in the liturgy. They unite people in responses.

Bulletins also announce other ministries beyond the Sunday morning worship hour. They list church family activities, community outreach, and world concerns.

And whether we like to admit it or not, *bulletins tell secrets about the church itself.* Paper grade, print type, writing style, neatness, and general impression help set the ambience for worship. They cue visitors to expect formality or informality, rigidity or creativity.

Having those common denominators, a few have introduced modifications. Consider the following, for instance:

Communion, Yes

The syndicated bulletin pictured a communion tray full of cups, lighted candle, a bunch of purple grapes, and a spray of wheat. "The cup of blessing . . . is it not the *communion*

Has the Church a Future? Westminster Press, 1980, p. 135.

of the blood of Christ?" 1 Corinthians 10:16 headlined the cover. This was Communion Sunday, without a doubt.

The inside pages, however, told another story. The text read like a friendly letter — all about exciting events of past and future. A newsletter, plus listing of pastors, flower donors, and candle-lighters. No order of worship.

We soon discovered that this non-liturgical church followed no set form. Music, sermon, announcements extended on and on. Communion ended a two-hour service.

Two Bulletins in One

Attend this interfaith church and you will receive identical bulletins the year around. Only the weekly insert changes.

The cover pictures the chapel steeple and entrance, etched in green ink on heavy, high-quality, white paper. The back of this permanent folder lists staff, board of governors, and fellowship organizations.

Inside, below an etched seal, this question appears:

What are our differences but keys to unlock the doors of understanding?

And following the order of worship, two short paragraphs reveal the spirit of the chapel:

All people are lovingly welcome into our interfaith Chapel. We are pleased to have you worship with us and ask that you come again.

Inter-faith: It is an open door through which anyone may pass and be understood; to share this faith with anyone else without fear of ridicule or censure.

The insert, of course, carries current announcements and liturgy details, like hymn numbers, anthems, and sermon subject.

This means the worshiper follows two bulletins throughout the service. However, the insert is a single sheet. This fact eases what could be a complicated shuffling of information.

The longest bulletin

Take a legal-size sheet of light bond paper. Fold it lengwise. Now you have a facsimile of the longest church bulletin we have encountered.

This unusual folding arrests attention. However, the long, narrow paper handles a bit awkwardly.

10" x 16" sheet persuades

A four-folded bulletin offers eight sides of purple print. It includes complete worship aids: hymn and anthem lyrics, responsive prayers and readings. No need for hymnals, except to follow notes.

"Opportunities This Week" fills a page. "Church News" follows, full of stimulating information concerning church and community action.

Over all, this format, its distinct print and many-faceted church program cannot help but impress newcomers. It reveals a lively, wide-scoped, caring Community of Believers. "Join us!" the bulletin pages shout (sophisticatedly, we might add).

Image shows through

Just barely can you make out the shadowy image of the church building. It appears as part of the paper on which Shadyside Presbyterian Church is printed in old English lettering.

Also atop the faint image on the bulletin cover for Easter Sunday are these words by Phillip Brooks:

The great Easter truth is not that we are to live newly after death — that is not the great thing — but that we are to live here and now by the power of the resurrection; not so much that we are to live forever, as that we are to live nobly now because we are to live forever!

What is the church's status?

Because church policy, creed, or denominational relationship rarely are spelled out in a bulletin, this Conregational Christian Church cover story we feature here. It clarifies many questions non-members might ask.

Printed in small, sharp type, this scenario appears under a photograph of the sanctuary interior.

"This church is a member of the United Church of Christ, a denomination of two million brought about in 1957 by a merger of the Evangelical and Reformed with Congregational Christian churches. A distinguished heritage dates back to Protestant reformation of the 16th century, and to early American Pilgrim Fathers in 1620. Our emphasis: Faith, Freedom, and Fellowship in Christ, local church autonomy and ecumenical church relationships."

Cover relates to sermon

A pen and ink drawing of a suspension bridge decorated the bulletin cover. It coordinated with the sermon subject: "Gap Bridges in a World of Gaps."

Bulletins actuate

What makes your church worth joining? The morning worship services give clues to the newcomer, to be sure. Also clues come from the bulletin pressed into the visitor's hand.

At best, it evangelizes. It stimulates further investigation and participation in fellowship and outreach. Your bulletin freely advertises the church's commitment to God's plan and people's needs. It aids worship; it maps concerns.

Examples of church programs and outreach that show creativity and awareness, I have gleaned from a couple hundred bulletins. They show *unusual* church activities only, since this book deals with innovations.

• Thursday: Blood pressure will be taken free of charge in the church library.

• *Travel club.* If you are interested in joining a travel club, please join us for an organizational meeting. We will discuss areas of interest and places to visit. Join us and become a charter member.

• The *"Green Thumbers"* are a group of faithful parishioners who groom the beautiful church campus every Friday. You may want to join them for this important ministry and fine fellowship.

• *Law of the Sea Seminar.* The Law of the Sea is considered to be one of the most critical of our day. Yet few people understand its importance. For those who wish to become better informed, there will be a seminar . . .

• *Redemptive Concern for Persons Affected by Crime.* Registration forms are available for the workshop on concern for persons affected by crime. Keynote speaker will be United Methodist Theologian, Harold DeWolf . . .

• *Casino Gambling.* Four years ago an attempt to legalize casino gambling in Florida was defeated, largely because of the opposition brought by the churches of the state. Now the churches of Florida are again being challenged to oppose casino gambling. On May 16, "special offering" envelopes will be in the pew pockets so we may receive an offering to finance the efforts to defeat this attempt to bring casino gambling to Florida . . .

• *You are invited to the Summer Doldrums Luncheon!* . . .

—————

• We welcome our *Cambodian Family*. Many members of our congregation and other friends of Say went to the airport with him to welcome Say's family who arrived Wednesday evening. It was a touching, heart-warming time . . . You may wish to send them letters or cards of welcome.

—————

• This morning the assistant is playing the organ and directing the choir. Our regular organist/choir director is taking this opportunity to sit in various locations in the congregation to "observe" acoustics of the organ and choir.

—————

Saturday, Senior High Social.
• FANTASTIC FEBRUARY'S FABULOUSLY FUNNY FILMS FESTIVAL IN FISK HALL WITH FOOD, FUN, FELLOWSHIP, FLICKS AND FRIENDS, AND IT'S FREE!

—————

• We have many willing workers for those odd jobs around the house — windows that need washing, leaky faucets, general house-cleaning, yardwork or whatever your need might be. Please give us a call.

—————

• The president of Physicians for Social Responsibility will be speaking at the Coalition for Survival meeting at the First Congregational United Church of Christ on Thursday.
    If you consider "Peace" to be the Christian primary concern, plan to attend.

- Twig Benders Class meets at 9:00 a.m.

- The Cancer Rap Group will meet Thursday at 4 p.m. in the church library.

- *Remember,* the church van goes to the grocery store each Thursday afternoon around one o'clock. Why not come to lunch at Congregate Dining and go shopping afterward? Just call the church office for home pick-up.

- *Storytellers and Friends.* Meeting Tuesday in church library. Storytelling is an old art and has recently been revived. Due to many inquiries in this area, a meeting time has been set for discussion concerning development, promotion, training skill sessions and festival plans. (A storyteller may make up a story, revive one from memory, or learn one from a book.)

- Mid Hi Human Sexuality Short Course meets Monday at 8 p.m.

- *Thanksgiving Service*: First United Methodist Church, together with Peace Memorial Presbyterian Church, will hold a joint Thanksgiving service . . . *Thanksgiving Dinner* will be served after the worship service . . .

- Today is our senior minister's *birthday*! Won't you wish him a good day? (They did. The congregation sang "Happy Birthday" during announcement time in the worship service.)

• Our *Christian Magazine TV Program* is every Friday evening from 7:00-7:30 on Channel 22.

• *Christmas Greetings.* We are planning a supplement sheet for the December *A CALL* to enable members to greet fellow members easily and economically. A greeting of three lines will be available for $5.00. *Save postage and support the A CALL.* Sample below:

Peace to you and yours. John Doe	Love came down at Christmas. Jane Doe

---

Seder Meal tickets are available at the foyer table for this Thursday evening Passover Meal. (United Methodist Church)

• Our church offers the community Drive-Thru Nativity Scenes. From seven to nine o'clock on the two weekend nights before Christmas, we invite the public to cruise slowly past these living tableaux.

Five-foot, hand-painted scrolls will stand beside the players. The lettering will identify each scriptural reference.

Over fifty people, of all ages, will pose as biblical characters. Two hundred candles will light the path through Bethlehem.

• "A Walk through Bethlehem" will take place this afternoon under the church porticoes. You and your friends are invited to visit the market place and the Holy Family. Try your hands at making pots, weaving baskets, carving wood, and petting animals.

Mingle among the Bethlehemites and Romans, as they toss bits of Scripture into conversation. Listen to the gossip and share the exciting news about the new baby. Visit that baby in the stable.

The Roman soldiers will be there, too. They will light the torches.

• Row, row, row your boat . . . It's that time of year again for our annual all-church canoe trip. It is set for Saturday. We will plan on leaving the church at 8:30 A.M. and canoeing 15 miles down the Peace River. Bring a lunch and plan on picnicking somewhere along the river. Please fill in the tear-out and place in the offering plate. Please, no children without adult supervision.

• *Persons Attending Worship Today* To Receive Palm Cross. Wear your handmade cross in remembrance of the suffering of our Lord and as a symbol of victory over death. Our special thanks to our youngsters and others for this labor of love in making these crosses.

• Did You Know
— Large print editions of the bulletin and hymnbook are available each Sunday?
— Wireless hearing aids allow you to sit any place in the sanctuary?
— Audio tapes are made of every sermon and may be borrowed or purchased?

Members Are Ministers

Pastor and *minister* usually are defined as synonyms. The Manasouan, New Jersey, First Presbyterian Church bulletin cover, however, distinguishes between the two terms.

Under the word Pastors appear the names of the clergymen. And below the word Ministers is printed:

All the members of the church.

Floral Cross a New Tradition at Trinity

On Easter Sunday a cross erected on the west front lawn will serve as an inspiration to all who see it. Members and visitors are invited to bring a fresh cut flower (with stem) and place it on the cross as they go into the Easter service.

Pew Cards Minister to Newcomers

Occasionally, creatively-composed welcome cards, tucked in pew pockets, reach out and touch visitors, caringly. Their messages actuate.

Here are two examples. Both register attendances. Beyond that, though, they inform the newcomer about church concerns.

Capsules church outreach

A three-by-six inch folder pictures the beautiful Southern Colonial edifice in color; the minister, in black and white. Inside listings reveal church ministries and questions about the visitor. The back of the perforated folder presents Deuteronomy 31:12. "Gather the people together, men, and women, and children, and the stranger that is within thy gates, that they may hear, and that they may learn, and fear the LORD your God, and observe to do all the words of this law:"

The perforated card allows the guest to turn in the information about self, at the same time saving the church photograph and spiritual ministries program to take home. (Note the two sections shown here.)

Wishes recorded

A sophisticated little folder (two by six inches) challenges the visitor to "Make a Wish" that will help improve the church program.

It includes the usual opportunities to help with church school, et cetera; to talk with the minister; to receive a pastoral call. Content, though typical, is packaged cleverly. (Note format in accompanying example.)

Pew Pocket Cards

West Bradenton Baptist Church has been serving Bradenton, the Beaches and Manatee County in many and varied ways since 1957 when it was organized. Some of the spiritual ministries are listed here:

BIBLE STUDY	for the WHOLE family — 8:30 & 9:45 AM — SUNDAY
WORSHIP SERVICES	9:45 & 11:00 AM, 7:00 PM — SUNDAY
PRAYER SUPPORT	7:00 PM — WEDNESDAY
MISSION EDUCATION	5:50 PM (children's groups) — WEDNESDAY FAMILY NIGHT SUPPER 5:15 PM
CHOIR PROGRAM	Children 4:30 PM, Adults 7:45 PM — WEDNESDAY Handbell Choirs, Orchestra
DISCIPLESHIP	Church Training for Family 6:00 PM — SUNDAY
YOUTH PROGRAM	Retreats, summer camps and Joy Explosion 7:00 PM — WEDNESDAY
RECREATION	Monday-Tuesday-Thursday-Friday-Saturday (Age Group)
GOLDEN AGERS	(Senior Adults) 10:00 AM (Lunch) — FRIDAY
REST HOME MINISTRY	Teams Minister to over 500 (9:00-11:30 AM) — SUNDAY
OUTREACH	Church-wide Visitation 7:00 PM — THURSDAY
DEAF MINISTRY	9:45 AM Bible Study, 6:00 PM Training (Interpretor at 11:00 AM and 7:00 PM) — SUNDAY
MISSION OUTREACH	Brazil, Haiti, Cooperative Program Channel 40 — WXLT-TV 10:00 AM — SUNDAY; Radio — WTRL — 11:00 AM SUNDAY

WBBC is a member of the cooperative efforts of Manatee, Florida and Southern Batist churches.

Getting to know you . . .

SINGLE
MARRIED

Mr.
Mrs.
Miss _____

NAME   DATE

_____
HOME ADDRESS   TELEPHONE

_____
CITY   STATE   ZIP CODE

WOULD YOU LIKE TO KNOW MORE ABOUT THIS CHURCH?_____

_____
PRESENT CHURCH MEMBERSHIP   S.S. MEMBER

PLEASE CHECK: (AGE GROUP OR GRADE)
18-21   22-25   26-29   30-34   35-39   40-44   45-59   60-80
12 11 10   9   8   7   6   5   4   3   2   1   PRESCHOOL
I AM A GUEST OF _____
HOW DID YOU HEAR ABOUT OUR CHURCH? TV RADIO NEWSPAPER FRIEND DRIVE-BY OTHER

Please Come Again

Pew Pocket Cards

How often have you sat in the pew of a church and have said to yourself —

"I WISH . . ."

We are always interested in improving the program and ministry of LONGBOAT ISLAND CHAPEL. Here is room for you to help by writing your suggestion of ways in which the effectiveness of the Church's program may be heightened. Check your wish, sign your name, and drop this folder in the offering plate or give to the Minister this morning.

[ ] I wish I could work with:
　[ ] The Church School
　[ ] A Youth Group
　[ ] The Women's Association
　[ ] The Choirs
　[ ] The Men's Group
[ ] I am a visitor and I wish to report my presence.

[ ] I wish I could get to know better some of the people of this church.
[ ] I wish I could talk to the minister sometime when convenient for both of us.
[ ] I wish I were a member of this congregation.
[ ] I wish I had some special task I could do in this church.
[ ] I wish the minister would call on _____

who is sick.
[ ] I wish that the minister would preach a sermon on
_____
_____

[ ] I wish I had offering envelopes
[ ] I wish _____
_____
_____
_____

Children in the Pew, Pamphlet in Bulletin

"Making Room for Children" helps parents and other members of the congregation adapt to the presence of children in worship. Parishioners discovered this special brochure tucked in their bulletins one September Sunday at Central Reformed Church, Grand Rapids, Michigan.

The folder projects the premise that bringing children to worship may not always be easy, but it is essential to their growth in Christ.

The first page lists activities the church provides for children during worship. They include the usual nursery, a children's time before they go to their own religious education sessions, and special festivals throughout the year. Also mentioned are worship activity bulletins and Bible story books for younger children. They may help themselves to these in the Narthex.

Another page describes what a pre-schooler brings to worship: short interest span, boundless energy, and growing curiosity. Then follow several suggested ways parents can make pre-schooler's (and their own) worship experiences more enjoyable. For example:

— Sit near the front, where the child can see.

— Explain parts of the service ahead of time, and answer questions when asked.

— Encourage the child to use the worship activity books (mentioned above).

— Allow the child to look at Bible story books or play with a stuffed animal brought from home, when bored.

The folder features the primary child next. Abilities outlined are longer listening span; increased reading, organizing, and memorizing skills.

Ways parents can help primaries participate in worship are:

— Encourage them to memorize the Lord's Prayer, Gloria Patri, and Doxology.

— Study the bulletin with them.

— Aid them in finding passages and numbers for Scripture reading, responses, and hymns.

— Talk about the sermon; ask questions.

Finally, the pamphlet lists what children may learn from attendance at worship. Also appears ABC's for parents and friends of children.

6. Physical Awareness

Ministry to the Deaf

• According to the bulletin, they attended a Sunday church school class for the deaf before eleven o'clock worship. That accounted for the group.

They entered from a side door and sat at the front right of the sanctuary. Throughout the entire service, a young woman stood in front of them, motioning in sign language all spoken and sung parts.

This is a regular ministry to the deaf each Sunday.

———————

• In a much smaller church, the deaf sat in the back two rows of one side of the worship room. The interpreter stood in the row in front of them, at the aisle.

Positioned this way, none of the congregation except those across the aisle watched the hand action. Visitors, alerted by an announcement in the newspaper about the program, missed the action. Sign language had become so much a part of the ritual that no mention was made about it.

A dozen people participated. They were all children and teenagers, except for one elderly man.

———————

Visually impaired worshipers at the Church of the Palms may request ushers bring them large print Bibles and hymnals.

———————

Caring for the Physically Handicapped

Steep stone steps lead up to the outside doors of the second-story sanctuary. They discourage heart bypass, arthritic, and physically handicapped worshipers.

Even fairly healthy visitors find the steps to be as forbidding as the Washington Monument stairway. No sign directs them to alternative routes.

However, this church does offer two easier entrances. On the right side of the building, a concrete ramp extends to the second floor level. Also farther back on the same side, an entrance opens on floor level. Both have double automatic doors.

To the right of the ground floor door is an elevator. Its automatic timer accommodates slow-moving passengers.

Whether they use ramp or elevator, physically handicapped worshipers may enter the front of the sanctuary. There they have space for wheelchairs, walkers, or crutches. Courteous ushers assist them.

Several churches provide wooden ramps alongside short stairways. But to build a two-story cement ramp requires major construction. And elevators cost dearly. Therefore, these architectural changes obviously reflect a people-concerned congregation.

Which brings to mind Harold A. Wilke's book, *Creating the Caring Congregation* (Abingdon). In it, Wilke lists practical steps that parishioners can take to serve the handicapped.

Posture Reversed in Worship

Reversing corporate posture sharpens awareness — for this pew-person, at least.

In an American Lutheran church, for instance, the congregation *sat* throughout the processional hymn. They *stood* during the pastoral prayer.

This turn-about from anticipated positions had its positive features. No one obstructed my view of the liturgical parade. And the pastor's petition pierced through my thoughts so sharply that I still remember his words.

For the congregation using this procedure every Sunday, these are "comfortable pew" postures. To stand for procession and sit for pastoral prayer likely would stab their sensitivities. For worship actions reversed seem to fine-tune audience awareness — until the novelty wears off. Then the old way becomes new again.

Standing to Worship

• The entire congregation *stood* throughout the worship service we attended at Cologne Cathedral. No seats were visible. People stood shoulder to shoulder. Hundreds of visitors (in the city for an international soccer game to be played later in the day) crowded the enormous nave.

Standing through prayers and sermon was a new experience for us. However, the no-pew concept has existed as far back in time as the the early Christian churches. Standing was the practice then. Only elderly and infirm sat on benches that lined the walls of the room.

Standing sharpened physical awareness of ourselves and our environment. Prior to this cathedral event, closeness in standing crowds we had experienced only at parades, malls, and games. In this service, though, invading each other's spatial intimacy seemed to highlight the corporate significance of worship. We felt a unity of spirit.

Permanent pews, however, forbid standing crowd closeness. Only by moving into an all-purpose room, gymnasium, or church dining room is open space found. And that's exactly what some innovative-minded ministers have done, to experiment with standing services.

• To give purpose to change of worship room, one pastor and worship committee recreated an early Christian service. Parishioners stood. The minister, though, delivered his sermon from a pulpit chair (reminiscent of the bishop's chair). By reverting back to early history, congregation and minister reversed worship postures for one Sunday.

• The pastor of a large Gothic-style church spontaneously changed to a standing service as an alternative one sub-zero morning. The heating system failed to function. In the sanctuary, outgoing breaths almost froze. Rather than cancel at the last minute, the minister moved the service into the church parlor.

A few people crowded the sofas. The majority, though, stood. In overcoats, mufflers, and gloves, they huddled together to keep warm.

Once again, standing changed perspective, sense of time, an awareness of liturgical acts. The *comfortable pew* was abandoned.

Several new churches capitalize on movable pews in their sanctuaries. Ecclesiastical furniture and fixtures (including the altar) may be moved to accommodate different types of worship. If your church design has central space, yours is the ideal setting for a *standing* service. Otherwise, why not move your congregation?

Changing the Pew View

"Be innovative yourself as a worshiper," challenged one pastor from his pulpit. "Try sitting in a different location in the sanctuary each Sunday for a month or two. You will be surprised at the novelty of the same service, viewed from other pews."

We know what he meant. For instance, in one church we visit frequently, we sat far to the right on the front row on Easter. (We had no choice.)

Gone was the symetrical center view we prefer. But we had added advantages. We saw the faces of choir members as they passed us. One line turned right at the chancel steps, so we had a frontal view before they turned left immediately in front of us to go up to the choir stalls.

We saw two ushers come forward during the singing of the last hymn. They carried the offering plates from the altar, past us, down the far right aisle. (They do this every Sunday, we have observed since then.) Their piles of plates looked so heavy. Would they make it to the rear, we wondered.

The young boy acolyte sat beside us. We watched him signal the little girl acolyte on the other side of the church. They walked toward each other, perfectly timed to meet at chancel-center.

Were these distractions? Not really. The intimacy of watching participants gave us a personal involvement in the service, unique to front pew seating.

Appendix

Positive Aids to Worship

Noted while church-hopping, are the following pluses, especially to aid visitors — and potential members.

- Outside church publicity is constant and visible.
1. A welcome sign, immediately in front of the church and seen from traffic lanes, labels the church and its hours of services.
2. Church name, address and hours of services appear in the telephone directory yellow pages.
3. Posted in hotel and motel lobbies is this same vital information, plus map directions for finding the church.
4. An informative advertisement appears on the local newspapers' church page.

- Trained personnel answer the church telephones on Sunday morning. They are ready with answers to such questions as: Who is preaching? Is there a nursery during worship hours? Is there a children's extended program while adults worship? Is communion being served?
- Ushers give bulletins to each worshiper, child and adult. (Too often a wife is expected to share her husband's bulletin and children are bypassed — an unintended type of discrimination.)
- The words "debts and debtors" or "trespasses and trespass" are printed in the bulletin, alongside the Lord's Prayer order.
- Members greet visitors who don identity tags. (Why wear a red ribbon if no one speaks to you?)
- Bulletins are easy to read in dim light.
- When house lights dim for the sermon time, a bright spotlight focuses on the pastor and pulpit.
- Audio crew pretested microphones, in order to minimize squealing, fading, and blasting sounds.
- Parishioners smile!
- Lay people assist the ministers in leading worship.
- The worshiper *feels* God's presence.

Newcomers Quizzed

Why do people come to worship in our church? Why do they stay — or leave? To answer these questions, six Episcopal parishes (in Indiana and Maryland) hired an outside organization to conduct a study for them.

The Álban Institute of Washington D.C. interviewed thirty-four to seventy-five newcomers in each church, whether or not they had joined. They orally answered forty-six questions and wrote responses to nineteen.

Among the positives they cited that are pertinent to morning worship were the following:

• The beauty and dignity of Episcopal services.
• Music (in three of the five churches).
• Strong lay leadership.
• Friendliness of the congregation.
• The clergy.

Weaknesses cited included:

• Lack of guidance and orientation to Episcopal worship.
• Little attention to special needs of transfers.

As a result of these parish-profiles, the six churches reportedly plan follow-ups to include:

• A new booklet about the parish.
• Name tags.
• Pew cards.
• Outdoor signs that list hours of services.
• Talks on mechanics of worship.

Reported in *Jed/Share*, Spring 1983, p. 27. Used by permission.

Acknowledgments

I give thanks to the innovators — ministerial and lay — who unknowingly made *Sunday Morning Alive!* Their enthusiasm and daring punctuated routine ritual with spiritual highs.

Special thanks goes to pastors who have given me permission to use excerpts and examples verbatim:

Doug Adams, Professor at Pacific School of Religion, Berkeley, California (Extra Bread Distributed).

George Brown, Jr., Central Reformed Church, Grand Rapids, Michigan (Children in the Pew Pamphlet in Bulletin).

John W. Eyster, Emerald Grove Congregational Church, Janesville, Wisconsin (Children Create Bulletin Designs, Teenagers Talk).

Charles Jim Marsh, Longboat Key Island Chapel, Longboat Key, Florida (Two Bulletins in One, I WISH pew pocket brochure).

Robert M. Rymph, First Congregational Church United Church of Christ, Bradenton, Florida (What Is the Church's Status?)

Maurice Stone, First Presbyterian Church, Sarasota, Florida (Walk-through Sculpture).

Larry V. Wells, Assistant Pastor, West Bradenton Baptist Church, Bradenton, Florida (Pew Cards Minister to Newcomers: Capsule church outreach).

Charles Whittle, First United Methodist Church, Abilene, Texas.

I am also grateful to lay friends for sharing creative acts they have witnessed: Franz Engel, Hatti Baribeau, Bonnie L. Fatio, Nancy R. Muenker, Betty Lee Santel, Deborah J. Phelps, Jessie Rega.

Copyrighted material which publishers have given me permission to use includes the following:

Why People Join the Church, An Expository Study, Edward A. Rauff, Pilgrim Press, p. 202.
The Comfortable Pew, Pierre Burton, J. B. Lippincott Company. Copyright 1965 by Pierre Burton. (Reprinted by permission of Harper & Row Publishers.)
The Ministry of the Child, Dennis Benson and Stan Stewart, Abingdon Press. Copyright by Dennis Benson and used by his permission.
Learning Through Liturgy, John Westerhoff, Seabury Press, 1978, p. 103.
Has the Church a Future? Douglas Hall, Westminster Press, 1980, p. 136.
"Religion and the Arts," Henry R. Luce II, *Yale Divinity School Reflections*, November 1981, Volume 70, No. 1, p. 6.
Introduction to Christian Worship, James F. White, Abingdon Press, 1980, p. 22.

Several ideas printed here first appeared in *Leadership*, Winter Issue 1982, Volume III, Number 1.

Reprint permissions for music include:

Extra verse of Old Hundredth Psalm, arranged by Ralph Vaugh Williams, Oxford University Press.
Musical score and stanza of "Rise, Shine," Augsburg Publishing House.

About the Author
An Afterword by Shirley Pollock

I have rarely missed a Sunday morning worship service. That's no idle boast. It's a fact, resulting from living in United Methodist parsonages — first as a preacher's kid, and later as a minister's wife. My religious heritage is rich. My religious environment is continual. To my Northwestern University School of Speech degree, I added religious education courses. At Yale Divinity School I audited classes, and at New College, University of Edinburgh, Scotland, I attended convocations (while my husband worked toward his Ph.D.). In the years that followed, in the local churches we served, I assumed the jobs no one else wanted. Summer camp directing and college Religious Emphasis Week counseling added religious highs to years of nurturing our four daughters.

My writing career began while my husband was a chaplain overseas. Hundreds of articles have been published since then — plus curriculum studies and six books.

My recent church-hopping venture to research *Sunday Morning Alive!* has stretched my own religious environment. I "caught the spirit," revealed through daring and different acts of worship. May you, the reader, catch the joy of creativity by adapting some of these spiritual ventures.